BY DAVID WAGONER

Poems

Dry Sun, Dry Wind (1953)
A Place to Stand (1958)
The Nesting Ground (1963)
Staying Alive (1966)
New and Selected Poems (1969)
Riverbed (1972)
Sleeping in the Woods (1974)
Travelling Light (1976)
Collected Poems 1956–1976 (1976)
Who Shall Be the Sun? (1978)
In Broken Country (1979)

Novels

The Man in the Middle (1954)
Money Money Money (1955)
Rock (1958)
The Escape Artist (1965)
Baby, Come on Inside (1968)
Where Is My Wandering Boy Tonight? (1970)
The Road to Many a Wonder (1974)
Tracker (1975)
Whole Hog (1976)

Edited

Straw for the Fire: From the Notebooks of Theodore Roethke,
    1943–1963 (1972)

IN BROKEN COUNTRY

❖❖❖

In Broken Country

Poems

DAVID WAGONER

An Atlantic Monthly Press Book
Little, Brown and Company — Boston – Toronto

B

LIBRARY OF CONGRESS CATALOGING IN PUBLICATION DATA

Wagoner, David.
    In broken country.

    "An Atlantic Monthly Press book."
    I. Title.
PS3545.A345I5   811'.5'4   79–13364
ISBN 0–316–91704–4
ISBN 0–316–91703–6 pbk.

ATLANTIC–LITTLE, BROWN BOOKS
ARE PUBLISHED BY
LITTLE, BROWN AND COMPANY
IN ASSOCIATION WITH
THE ATLANTIC MONTHLY PRESS

MV

Designed by Susan Windheim

Published simultaneously in Canada
by Little, Brown & Company (Canada) Limited

PRINTED IN THE UNITED STATES OF AMERICA

For Patt
and all the missing singers
with love

※※

CONTENTS

One

Two

❖

One

AFTER THE SPEECH TO THE LIBRARIANS

I was speaking to the Librarians,
And now I'm standing at the end of a road,
Having taken a wrong turn going home.
I don't remember what I said.
Something about reading and writing
And not enough about listening and singing.
The gate to this dude ranch is locked,
And a dozen riderless horses are browsing
On the hillside in the gold grass.
On a post, a marsh hawk is holding still,
One eye on me and one on the field
Where hundreds of sparrow-sized water pipits
Are darting and whistling to themselves.
Not even thinking of opening a thesaurus,
I say on behalf of the Librarians, *Beautiful*.

Beyond barbed wire, a cracked water tank
And a wrecked shed: you could wait there
A long time for a school bus.
Whoever locked the gate meant No Thank You,
Not Today, but it wasn't much use.
Everything is trespassing as easily
As the hazy sunlight and these burnt-gold-breasted birds
Taking their sweet time under the hawk's eye,
Even perching beside him, extremely happy
To be where they are and what they are,
And the horses with nothing on their backs
Have opened their own gates for the winter,

And the Librarians are going back to their books
In hundreds and hundreds of schools where children
Will be reading and writing and keeping quiet
Maybe and listening to how not to be so childish.

When I wasn't looking, the hawk flew suddenly,
Skimming the field, effortlessly graceful, tilting
And scanning at low-level: he stops
Dead without slowing down, swivels
And drops into the grass, flashing white
And tawny, rises at full speed carrying nothing
And goes on soaring, slanting downhill
No higher than my head, making his sharp outcry.
The water pipits answer, thin as fence-wire.
Isn't it wonderful not being dead yet?
Their breasts all hold the same air
As his and the softly whickering unsaddled horses'
And mine and the Librarians'
With which we all might sing for the children.

BOY JESUS

When they made me the boy Jesus
In the Sunday school Christmas pageant, oh Jesus,
I would have given almost anything
To be anybody else in the world but a made-up Jesus.

But suddenly it was too late to say anything
Polite against it or do anything
Desperate in my knee-length toga, while my squirming friends
Snickered in the pews, or even *feel* anything

As I floated down the endless aisle, praying those friends
Would forget someday and be real friends
And not remember me forever singing that damned song
In a shaky soprano, "All Men Be Loving Friends."

It would have been terrible enough singing any song
In public, even the school fight song,
But to have to look so holy-faced and fluttery while I,
Of all young sinners, sang it, made it my swan song.

Why had they picked on me? Jesus and I
Gave each other a pain: I couldn't stump preachers, could I?
No dove had come flapping down when I was baptized, I was no boy
Genius, and we were Laurel and Hardy carpenters, my father and I.

And my voice was breaking: I was only half a boy,
A sneak-thief, liar, prober of loveless keyholes, a would-be boy

Magician, a card-stacker more ruled by swear-words
Than by Jesus Christ Almighty, the Good Boy.

From that day on, I put my fidgety faith in my own words
And later in love — in ugly, profane, beautiful words,
Instead of going hook, line, and sinker for Jesus —
No Gospels for the Fishers of Men, but love in other words.

✖✖✖

JEREMIAD

The night I was Jeremiah
In the Sunday school panorama
Unravelling the Bible
From Exodus to Easter,
The Word of the Lord came unto me (memorized
In a cold garage
With no help from our Chrysler):
I was announcing Woe
Between Gary and Chicago
Where it was wonderful shouting
We could all be wiped out clean
By God some smoky morning.

The beard of this prophet
Was a black-crape botch-up
Whose gum had just enough spirit
To lose its place in the windy
Word of the Lord coming out of me slightly garbled
To tell those rows of pews
They'd be exceedingly massacred
While my robe of miscast curtains
Puffed dust into my ears,
A warning cloud from the wilderness
Of our attic, a parable
As dry as Israel's cisterns.

Isaiah softened them up
And then I let them have it,

And not even sweet Jesus
Who came on later could flatten
The Word of the Lord we'd rammed in first and loudest.
Since our feet didn't show,
All of us wise old prophets
Wore sneakers and sneaked out
Before the Crucifixion,
Still full of lost diatribes
As the Golden Rule's star turn
Ran smack into our Doomsday.

THE JUNIOR HIGHSCHOOL
BAND CONCERT

When our semi-conductor
Raised his baton, we sat there
Gaping at *Marche Militaire*,
Our mouth-opening number.
It seemed faintly familiar
(We'd rehearsed it all that winter),
But we attacked in such a blur,
No army anywhere
On its stomach or all fours
Could have squeezed through our crossfire.

I played cornet, seventh chair
Out of seven, my embouchure
A glorified Bronx cheer
Through that three-keyed keyhole stopper
And neighborhood window-slammer
Where mildew fought for air
At every exhausted corner,
My fingering still unsure
After scaling it for a year
Except on the spit-valve lever.

Each straight-faced mother and father
Retested his moral fibre
Against our traps and slurs
And the inadvertent whickers
Paradiddled by our snares,

And when the brass bulled forth
A blare fit to horn over
Jericho two bars sooner
Than Joshua's harsh measures,
They still had the nerve to stare.

By the last lost chord, our director
Looked older and soberer.
No doubt, in his mind's ear
Some band somewhere
In some Music of some Sphere
Was striking a note as pure
As the wishes of Franz Schubert,
But meanwhile here we were:
A lesson in everything minor,
Decomposing our first composer.

DIRGE FOR A PLAYER-PIANO

The trouble was we moved
So often, we couldn't be loaded
Down with that clunker, he said.
It would have to be half-gutted,
Leaving the manual keyboard
But cutting out what played
"Kiss Me Again" (pumped hard)
Like a band-cart in a parade.

So my father bent over the coffin
For days, struggling to loosen
Whatever was hanging on
To "My Bonnie Lies Over the Ocean,"
Unscrewing and chiselling
And finally crowbarring
Those heavyweight labyrinthine
Innards out in the open.

And what a heap it was:
Long tubes and resplendent levers,
Three-angled brassy brackets,
Mahogany sandwiches
With nothing inside, enough screws
To turn home-carpenters
Through three inscrutable winters
But nothing like "Wang-Wang Blues."

My brother and sister once
Had taken terrible lessons

On that hollow mourner's bench.
When my turn came, it was nonsense
(*Ponderoso doloroso fervente*)
To waste some more thin dimes
Under clocks by metronomes
On "Liebestraum" and "Narcissus."

But I'd loved watching the keys
Sink under no one's claws
In such faultless clusters
And *sforzando* arpeggios,
While my prodigious toes
Trod floods of "Beautiful Ohio"'s
And sand dunes of "Araby"'s
Till those wonders rolled to pieces.

My father played by ear,
Not feet, so it didn't matter
If my slewfoot shows were over,
But eighty-eight keys still bar
Me from the lost ghost-fingers
Of "Ramona" and "Dardanella"
And "Marcheta," now forever
Holes wound up in paper.

MY FATHER'S WALL

The old one was falling: the cracked gravelly pieces flaking
Like a good start on a ruin down the steep driveway
Into our basement garage. My father (stonemason
Self-taught) and I (apprentice to other sorcerers)
Slapped up the ship-lap form with soleplates and raking shores
Sawed out of foundling lumber. When the truck backed in
With two yards of ready-mix jumbling in its drum
And the chute swung over, we thought we'd be all set.

The bulges started low — planks springing out like strakes
And a gray mass surging and slobbering at our ankles —
And as he braced and yelled and improvised, I shovelled
What leaked below back over that unmanned barricade
Again and again, but it flushed down through six feet of baffles
Faster than I could keep it up. I'd shovelled coal and cinders,
Sand and dirt, even manure in my meagre time, but nothing
That had wanted to be somewhere else and something else so badly.

Gradually the mess thickened and slowed, and more stayed in
Than ran away. It put up with our planks, now only dripping
Through the sprung seams, and while our overalls hardened
Into permanent contortions like war-memorial drapery
And our feet grew heavier inside their concrete boots,
We left it to bleed all night without us. But in my sleep
I listened for all four tons to break loose, rumbling down-slope
To the garage, a solid, no-nonsense, no-passenger family tank.

MY FLYING CIRCUS

Having missed a great World War,
I made those model planes
And dreamed of flying
A Nieuport, a Sopwith Camel,
A Spad, an Albatross,
Even a three-winged Fokker.
I sanded and cut corners,
Enamelled, glued, and strutted
Red-handed as Richtofen.

In my goggle-eyed daydreams
We climbed through harmless flak
And dove out of the sun
On our delightful foes,
All starry as football heroes.
Whether we killed or were killed,
We went grinning down in flames,
White scarves trailing like plumes
Of smoke in easy slipstreams.

They hung from my bedroom ceiling
By the slenderest of threads
Like marionettes of birds
And flew all night, going nowhere
Fast in the No Man's Land
Of my head under a pillow
Where I floated half in a cloud,
And their silent engines

And innocent machineguns
Stalled and hung-fire till dawn.

I never got off the ground
With the likes of them. They crashed
Somewhere long ago:
One day their sky went blank
As it suddenly dawned on me
Real Aces hang from nothing,
Real Dawn Patrols come back
To earth, burning in streaks
As gloriously as fireworks.

✖✖✖

PART SONG

At the nursing home's Thanksgiving party
The janitor is singing "Trees"
Better than anyone could have hoped for.
All of us, old and older, are shedding leaves.

He sings in a heart-failed baritone
As if he meant each lame, unlikely word,
And all of us are changing color
Over tea and cookies and clumsy conversation.

As if I'd meant each lame, blind, halting word
Long ago, I'm choking over my lost mother
Over coffee and cake and vacant conversations.
She used to sing it better than I expected.

And here I'm choking over my grandmother
And my wife beside her and all the missing singers.
We used to live as well as we could hope for.
We used to sing in the morning like young robins.

My wife beside herself and the missing singers
Applaud when "Trees" is over, whispering thank you.
We used to sing in our cages like starved robins.
Now we sit still, not looking at God all day.

When the applause dies down, we're mumbling thank you,
Thank you for singing anything, even that.

Now some sit still as God, making no trees.
All their gray mouths lie open as if singing.

God, thank them for singing anything, even nothing.
The snow on their bosoms drifts a little further.
All their gray mouths lie open for more snow.
The earth's sweet breast is flowing away from them.

INTO THE NAMELESS PLACES

"Mr(s) _____ is undergoing Reality Orientation to help
him/her remember who and where he/she is. Please include
the following questions in your conversation with him/her."
— notice on a nursing home wall

Your name is?

Not on the tip of my tongue, but slipping away
And only half-returning when I call it
To mind, to mind me like a child
As it used to when I recited it
More clearly and easily than any other answer.
It waits shyly, a little way off, uncertain
Whether it must come back to touch my lips
Or whether I'll follow it slowly in good time
Into the nameless places it longs for.

The date is?

All of the hundred, all of the twelve,
All of the thirty, the seven, the twenty-four,
All of the sixty, all of the sixty.

The weather is?

On the other side of the window where it waits
Or wanders, either a blurred brightness
Or a blurred gray through which everything rises
That wants to rise, then gathers to rise
Again, out of reach, beyond me, without me.

Tomorrow is?

As it may be or as it was
Yesterday, and ever shall be in the beginning
Of sleep and the end of waking, both meeting
Like upper and lower eyelids, as silently

As eyelids rising and falling, lashes touching
In the calm storm of the darkness.
Your birthday is?
       This morning again, and again the years
       Repeating themselves as fervently as wishes,
       The many happy returns of wax and smoke
       Like my breath passing away over the face
       Of sweetness, layer by layer, crumbling, breathless.
You were born in the city of?
       In the walled city of a hospital among nurses
       And hands and sheets where all the furniture
       Rolls slowly away over the bare floors,
       And my sainted aunts surround me
       With murmurous attention, all but one:
       The dark lady-in-waiting whose needle
       Sews up the doors and windows, gives this castle
       The long rest of its life, its retiring beauty,
       And no one asks me what the music means
       Coming from the walls, the music ending
       Only when the lights go dim. It sings
       In place of my voice, keeping time and never
       In need of any reminder to be over
       In order to make room for the next beginning,
       And no one asks if I wish to be
       Anyone else or called anyone younger
       Or where these rootless flowers have come from,
       What gardens must still be growing somewhere
       To pour such color against colorless pillows
       Or why everyone is too far away
       To kiss me, so lost beside me,
       Even inside my arms, and no one
       Asks out of politeness why I stare at nothing
       As if it were really here.

SONGS MY MOTHER TAUGHT ME

In a small throaty soprano
In perfect pitch always,
She sang "Thou Art Repose"
Before my feet could touch
The floor from the music bench
And "The Trout" — Schubert at peace
With his mildest remembrance,
Then glittering with fear.
I remember listening, awed
That her fingers touching the keys
(Too small to reach octaves)

Could clear a way for her voice
To stream through such music
Composed by real composers
Who had used just pen and ink
(A skill I'd halfway mastered
By scrawling words, not notes),
All dead, all living again
Each time she played and sang
"On Wings of Song," "Pale Hands
I Loved," "*Ich liebe dich*,"
"None But the Lonely Heart."

Now like Franz and Felix,
Amy, Edvard, and Piotr,
She depends on someone else

To sing what she dreamed of.
She has gone to her long rest
By the restless, restful waters
Of whatever Shalimar
Or Ganges she longed for
In Zeit und Ewigkeit,
Her heart no longer lonely,
And I sing this for her.

✖✖✖

THE SINGERS

> "Lend no ear to those that advise you to practice with
> a smile. It becomes set, and one never gets rid of it."
> — MATHILDE MARCHESI,
> "Correct Methods of Vocal Study"

Others may smile and smile, forgetting to try
To smile but always smiling, at our service,
The comic masks running and running for office,
Or those running from office to office, their lips
Turned up at the busy corners, or the speechless lovers
Smiling at fortune, even the ballerina
Persuading us her labors are pure joy,
All beamed by the glistening skin of their teeth
Hopefully into a climate of agreement.

But not the singers. Without false promises,
Leaving their smiles for later, lifting their voices
With calm, straight faces, they must face their music.

THE DEATH OF THE MOON

Through the long death of the moon, we drank her light
As slowly as snow-melt, bearing her funeral
Against the turn of the earth by nights like flares
As she fell westward, trailing a torn shroud
Across the mountains, over the ashen water.

Our feet washed pale as shell, we faltered
After her, naming all she could answer,
But she turned her cold, lopsided face
Further away than we could follow.

She shrank to half a skull,
Sinking as if to sleep
At the salt edge of her grave.

Then her white knife,
Her closing eyelid.

Her darkness.

xxx

THISTLEDOWN

A tuft of thistledown
Comes floating through the window
Of my parked car. It hovers
Between me and the mirror,
As light as the air
I have just stopped breathing,
A plumed cluster holding
One seed like its own breath;
Then in a down-draft
It mulls over nylon pile
And two shades of veneer
For a sign of one bare inch
Of earth, finds nothing, rises
And touches my inhospitable
Shirtfront, slowly traverses
My face without a lifeline
Like a ghost in a spider's nightmare,
Then skims back out the window
Past the bristling barbs
And the armed green jagged bracts
Of its elders, the bursting purple
And gray crowned heads
Whose roots have interlocked
Against all comers searching
For a share of the summer.

CLOUDBURST

When the sky burst, I was caught far down the treeless meadow
Beside a river rushing no harder now than the rain
Drenching the slope as if all air, out of its airy bluster,
Had changed half into water and fallen, end over cloudy end.

It beat the bushes and reeds and me and thistles and rushes
And shook and shivered us all, pelting the smooth river
And pouring till I was a gaping salmon under a waterfall
Stunned and stranded on moss. Then abruptly it ended.

And there in the newly made, steaming, streaming sunlight
The black-and-gilt goldfinches came to the thistle crowns,
Dipping and lilting with their interrupted wingbeats
From flowerhead to purple flowerhead half-gray with seed,

Zigzagging short and quick as moths and clinging sideways
To the stalks till both bent upside down, spilling over
And over their one brief call for each other to seek and find
Everywhere whatever they wished for under their gold father.

I held as still as a bittern or a stump, waiting to learn
Anything: they paid me no more mind than the rain
As they fed and darted away over the prickly, impassable field,
Singing, leaving me heavy-footed and bare-handed.

ELEGY WHILE PRUNING ROSES

"What saint strained so much,
Rose on such lopped limbs to a new life?"
— THEODORE ROETHKE

I've weeded their beds, put down manure and bark dust.
Now comes the hard part: theoretically
It has to be done, or they spend their blooming season
In a tangle of flowerless, overambitious arms.
So here go pruning shears in spite of the thorns
That kept off browsers for all the millennia
Before some proto-dreamer decided roses
Were beautiful or smelled their unlikely promise.

Reluctantly I follow the book and stunt them
In the prescribed shapes, but throwing cuttings away
Over the fence to die isn't easy.
They hang onto my gloves and won't let go,
Clutching and backlashing as if fighting
To stay in the garden, but I don't have time or patience
To root them in sand, transplant them, and no room
In an overcrowded plot, even supposing
They could stand my lame midhusbandry.
So into limbo with all these potential saints.

Already the ladybugs, their black-dotted orange
Houses always on fire, are climbing for aphids,
And here come leaf-rollers, thrips and mildew
To have their ways. I've given up poison:

These flowers are on their own for the spring and summer.
But watching the blood-red shoots fade into green
And buds burst to an embarrassing perfection,
I'll cut bouquets of them and remember
The dying branches tumbling downhill together.

Ted, you told me once there were days and days
When you *had* to garden, to get your hands
Down into literal dirt and bury them
Like roots to remind yourself what you might do
Or be next time, with luck. I've searched for that mindless
Ripeness and found it. Later, some of these flowers
Will go to the bedside of the woman I love.
The rest are for you, who weren't cut off in your prime
But near the end of a long good growing season
Before your first frost-bitten buds.
You knew where roots belonged, what mysterious roses
Come from and were meant for: thanks,
Apology, praise, celebration, wonder,
And love, in memory of the flourishing dead.

THE GIFT

Dear, now you have unfolded
This as you unfolded me:
We were both creased and cramped
Without your fingers,
But here we stretch in the light
Of your most frightening birthday,
Hoping you can forget
Those days, those days
When all you asked as a gift
Was not wanting to die.
I must remember always
Your quick blue eye
That follows each quick feather
The birds turn to the sun,
Your beautiful hopeless fists
Raised against the knives
And guns and steel teeth
That lie in wait for love,
Your phantasmagorical heart
Ready to pour its answer
Through small worlds left for dead —
All gifts you were born with
And have earned over and over
And carry now skin deep
And deeper forever.

FOR A WOMAN WHO SAID HER SOUL WAS LOST

You wept past midnight like a ghost in an old novel,
Haunting a room, a stairway, a whole house with your half-dreaming
Pain, inconsolable, unable to hear me. Love, I confess
I took your soul into the woods, into the mountains
Early this morning, climbed a steep path with it,
Cold and deserted, stood with it among swordferns
And blossoming red currant where, together, we heard the wrens
And ruby-crowned kinglets reclaiming their worlds
From the melting winter as certainly as moonrise
While your lost body, miles away, wandered among doctors.
Sleep soundly, slowly, and softly now. Your soul is waiting
Here in safekeeping through a long, disembodied nightwatch.

LOOKING UP

On the narrow spit, we lay among driftwood
In the sunlight, though the cold wind streamed above us
Only a foot away. In that bone-white shelter
We held each other, our gestures not yet made
Graceful or permanent by the weather.

No yard of sand we could see around us
Was without its empty shell or its bleached feather,
Its birdbone or tuft of barely living sedge.
At length, we lay beside ourselves, our faces
Turned to a winter sky, vacant of love.

And across it suddenly low enough to touch
If we had lifted our arms, their long necks stretching
Forward toward calm water, their wings whistling
In the wind more than the wind, in their own wind,
Hundreds of geese swept over and over us.

xxx

WATCHING THE HARBOR SEALS

They float erect, their heads out of the water,
And then slip under
Gently without a ripple, feeding together
And moving near the shore
Of Dungeness Bay at the bright end of summer,
The blue-green shimmer
Of sea-bedded sky and sky-bedded sea the color
Of both, of neither,
Of what lies lost in our eyes like the birth of weather,
And the gulls hover
Above this drifting feast of eleven harbor
Seals, long-calling over
The cormorants diving among them, every fish-catcher
Silent, each scavenger
Screaming and turning, the glistening fur
And each glistening feather
In its place under the sun. The seals' eyes stare
Toward us without fear,
Mildly and calmly, knowing what we are:
The ones who suffer
There on the dry stones in the empty air
From a different hunger,
Who stand and wait, who simply watch and wonder,
Holding each other.

※※※

FOR A WOMAN WHO DREAMED
ALL THE HORSES WERE DYING

You saw them falling in fields beyond barbed wire,
Their forelegs buckling, the horses kneeling
In the dead grass, then falling awkwardly
On their flanks to finish breathing
Where stems give way to roots under the earth
That will let no hoofprints last for a whole season,
Their eyes still staring, but sightless now, their withers
        Still, their long tails still.

You saw the empty trails, the stolid, bewildered
Cattle milling and shifting, turning
To gaze at four distances where no one
Was riding among them, saw empty harness
And reins trailing in dust, and the tongues
Of wagons empty, destined for nowhere
On an open plain, the crossfire of the wind
        Riddling the scattered bones.

And they were dead then, all of them everywhere,
You told me, dead and never to return.
Love, I offer my own brief dream: together
We wait in an unfenced field, and slowly
Shying along the hillside, the small wild horses
Come walking toward us, their unshod hooves
Tentative on the ground. Warily they stretch
        To muzzle our trembling hands.

LOVE SONG AFTER A NIGHTMARE

Half listen, love, half asleep,
To the beginning of morning:
Your dream was the water,
And over its face, light air
Comes singing out of the shadows
Across a field to our house:
Birdsong and one shred
From the buried nest of the sun
Entering (dim and distant)
This room where you have spent
All you could spend on the night
And now lie empty-handed.

Your hobbled heart, heartbeaten
Through the terrible pasture,
Not led but driven
Straight to the still water
And under, now falters ashore
Out of your nightmare
Still breathing, still carrying
The burden of its proof:
You, with your fear behind you.

Though the sun may burn
Among crossed branches
At the grate of the window
Like our bodies around our bones,
Love has come back alive

33

To stretch its arms again:
It will need nothing more
Than what we bring together
On this, our next first day
On earth, to make its garden.

Two

ELEGY FOR A MINOR ROMANTIC POET

If that's you gesturing frantically
Behind the cage-bars of your poems
To be let loose in a world you lost, I'm sorry:
Your work is dimming down to its late evening,
Maybe to its night, and your worst fears —
Being unknown and unread — apparently have come true.
The played-out play of your fancy
(Which seems as bound as you were determined)
Has faded further, dwindling
Nearly to sleep among thousands of others
Who led the way downward for the rest of us.

Once you scurried to act as outpost-keeper
For your dispirited neighbors, flaunting
Dozens of hats, growing outlandish mustachios,
Drinking and sleeping around and around
As faithfully as you could hope to, letting your hair
Flow with the prevailing wind, your fame
As sure as you were a prophet without honor
In anyone's country. Now critical eyes
Have decided *real* poetry is something different.
You stand on shelves where no one lifts a finger.

That painful message you kept urging the world
To heed! with exclamation points and *fervent italics*,
With all the embellishments that EMPHATIC FOUNTS could offer,
Has proved painless. The world didn't listen
To anyone who loved words, preferring

The emptily self-laden, self-devastating speeches
Of its Misrulers or, better yet, speechless abominations.
Your world consists, at an uninformed estimate,
Of seven substandard graduate students, anxious
To be sheepskinned and then done with
Everything you collected and recollected.

Your love was probably as beautiful
As you say she was, as imposing,
As heat-resistant in her flowery way,
But no one seems to care since you didn't
Sing her to life, transform her to Earth Mother,
Madonna, or Bitch Goddess. I'm afraid
I have to share the opinion that she lies
As stiff in print as in her coffin,
Yet I won't keep a scholar's indifference.

I'm reading you tonight with care and fear,
Stirring who knows what ghosts and skullduggery
In the backs of our two skulls, both grinning forward
At what may come from all this windy dust.
I'm glad you lived and tried to answer your calling.
What welled up in your eyes, what you found
Down the echo-filled well of your inspiration
Where moss and a few frogs had taken their damp comfort
Was worth more than the getting-and-not-spending
Or the spending-while-not-getting
You might have mastered in other disguises.

In those hard hours when language wouldn't behave,
When words — those miserable three-faced watchdogs —
Wouldn't perform their duties outdoors or in,
At shaky midnight or still shakier morning,
You bit both hands that fed you
And rapped your forehead and stained your foolscap
With tears and other unmanageable liquors
And felt at last you had beaten your way
Through, into a suddenly sweet light-dazzled clearing
Where no one had ever been, where the genuine magic

Of the ingenuous imagination
Had covered you with such a downfall of blossoms
You would never again be merely those doubtful selves
You had caught in hundreds of embarrassing postures
In all the mirrors you could possibly hold up to your nature.
Time says you were wrong. That illusion
You took to your grave like a hank of lover's hair
Must lie in wait like the spider silk I found stitching together
The uncut pages of your life.

BOOK SALE — FIVE CENTS EACH!

On the Salvation Army's bookshelves, the derelicts
Line up as if for coffee,
Some stuck together like doughnuts, some mumbling music
To warm up charity:
The soaked hymnals, the self-devotional memoirs
Droning Vanity, Vanity,
The loud reports from the Corporals of Industry
Now muffled by mildew,
The Rover Boys strung far Out West, blind-canyoned
By a ripped-off chapter,
And the backs of the books-of-the-month-after-month
Humped undercover,
The indigestible digests, the spiral schoolbooks
Telling and telling
What they're going to tell, then telling, now telling no one
What they told each other —
Rank after rank gone by the reviewing stand
To join this cold Army,
For hire, five cents forever, cheaper than kindling
If it comes to burning.
But *Laugh with Leacock* and *Laughing Boy* and *Memento Mori*,
All Quiet on the Western Front,
Come as you are, with dust on your riddled jackets,
Though your wounds need binding,
Oh, *Adam and Eve and Pinch Me, Beau Geste*, and *Victory*,
Come home to dinner.

ODE TO THE MUSE ON BEHALF
OF A YOUNG POET

Madam, he thinks you've become his lover. He doesn't know
            You're his landlady,
The keeper of the keys to the front door, the mistress
Of the stairwell, postmistress, indifferent cook, shade-lifter
Veiled by twitching curtains, protectress of thermostats,
            Handmaiden of dust.

He doesn't see your crowsfeet or cracked smile or the grayness
            Swept from your temples.
To him, your odor of mothballs is the heady essence
Of the Gardens of Inspiration and your bed-ridden houseplants
The Garden itself. Look, he has begun to scribble.
            Grant him your mercy.

If you should tell him he's behind in his rent instead,
            You may startle him
Out of a year's growth of beard and spirit. Consider
Your reputation, not as a bill-collector, but as the sole
Distributor of Sparks, Flashes, and Sudden Leaps
            From the Visionary Aether.

His heart's in the right place: in his mouth. If he means
            Anything, he means well.
If he means nothing to you, why not amuse him for a brief
Lifetime with the benefit of your doubt? What would you be

Without him and his attentions but an empty housekeeper,
A closet hostess?

Who else could be more ardent, more flattering? Already
He's wondering where you are.
He's inventing enough implausible, brilliant rivals to last you
Forever. He wouldn't dream of asking you to wash
His unmentionable linen or scrub his floor or thaw his dinner.
He's starving for you.

Blank paper pays you no honor. Using your name in vain
Is his only blasphemy.
Go to him now in disguise and comfort him with all
Your charm-filled anger, your dreadful, withering beauty,
Your explosive silences, the consolations of horror,
The forgeries of death.

✹✹✹

STUNTS

1. "Chair Crawl"

Materials: A strong kitchen chair.
Preparation: Sit on chair facing front. Lie
on your right side on seat, facing the
back, grasping back of chair with hands.
Stunt: Attempt to crawl around
back of chair, head and shoulders lead-
ing, and regain original sitting position
in seat. This is to be accomplished with-
out touching any part of body to floor.
— *A Handbook of Stunts,*
MARTIN RODGERS

Instead of sitting there
Unemployed, out of character,
With your shoes mislaid on the floor
And your ears in an uproar,
Even your indecorous rear
Ending its best behavior
At your antisocial lumbar
Region, stiff as that chair,
Why not choose to lie down
On the right side to begin
Making your way around
The back-rest that holds your spine
Hostage, hand over rung
Or groin under backhand,
One stunted hip for a cushion

And one knee catch-as-catch-can,
Till the uniqueness of your position
Seems almost as certain
As the snowflake of your soul
Whose suddenly chilling lesson
Through this unassisted horizontal
Self-contained constitutional
Should lead you to return
From circling the Back of Behind
(If you're strenuously stubborn)
As an upright citizen
Once more, a downright companion
Refreshed and refreshing,
Prepared to hold up your end
Of the nearest conversation
Definitely on your own.

2. "Head Push"

Materials: A wall.
Preparation: Draw a short line two foot-lengths from wall. Toe this line. Using hands, lean forward, and place top of head against wall. Now fold arms behind back.
Stunt: Push up to erect standing position, without displacing feet.

— *Ibid.*

You might have had any normal
Relationship with a wall:
Being backed up against it
Or trying to scramble over
Or hammering it or staring
At its dependable blankness,
But now, having chosen
This poor-man's, broad-based,
Blunt-instrumental headstand,
You will have time to learn
(Phrenologically speaking)
How much more agreeable
You would feel as a blockhead:
This plane is disinclined
To yield to your bumpy temples
Or your frontal eminence
(Ideality and Wit)
And offers only cold comfort
From your crown to your squared feet,
And in your case, which hinges
On your head instead of your hands,
If push won't come to shove,
You may take new lumps for old.

3. "Lead Feet"

Materials: A companion.
Preparation: Stand perfectly stiff, feet to-
gether. Press thumb and index finger of
each hand against sides of temples,
keeping elbows down and close to body.
Stunt: Have companion try to lift
you off the floor by the elbows.

— *Ibid.*

Ordinarily when you're standing
You're simply standing
Around, thinking of nothing,
Assuming no particular
Imposture of any kind,
Your feet paying no attention
To your hips or your haunches
Or the decline of your solar plexus,
But here comes your temptation:
This red-faced companion
Straining against you, crouching
Under your rigid elbows
To heist you out of your foot-sure
Stance, your perfect composure,
Won't know you're giving in
At the knees (where the secret lies
For holding your own ground),
Yet the rules of good clean fun
Require you to seem to stiffen
Helpfully, though you're cheating,
Meaning to stay a problem
By keeping your weight leaden
From diaphragm to breadline,
From ham to hock to heel
Grinding into the floor,
So no matter how headstrongly,
Heartstrongly, or gamely
The Other takes you on,
You're set for a let-down.

4. "Stand the Stiff"

Materials: A light companion.
Preparation: Have companion lie fully ex-
  tended on back, body absolutely rigid,
  hands outside of thighs. Stand on left
  side of body, bend down and place one
  hand under neck.
Stunt: Lift straight up to a stand-
  ing position (as though made of wood).
                        — *Ibid.*

Though this body, lying
Strait-laced at your feet,
Seems distant and uninviting,
Lock-kneed and tight-lipped,
Eyes turning away from you
Toward the ceiling or the insides
Of fitfully clenched eyelids,
It will (if you'll stoop to it)
Come heeling up at a fulcrum
All of a piece, free-standing,
A shipless figurehead
Or a houseless housepole,
Posing for you once more
Pygmalion's problem
Whose solution was as obvious
As moving and breathing:
Your hand below the neck
Lightly, light-heartedly,
Your arms coming up from darkness
Toward a light companion.

5. "Novelty Walk"

Materials: None.
Preparation: Stand, toeing a line, feet to-
gether, hands on hips.
Stunt: Carry right foot around be-
hind left and place it as far forward on
that side as possible. Now carry left be-
hind, alongside, and forward of the
right foot. Continue this cross-forward
walk indefinitely.

— *Ibid.*

Though heavy thinkers
May think the struggle
To get along
Is already random
Enough without this
Incongruous foot-boggling,
Get on with it,
Dipping off balance
Because you feel
Crotchets of novelty
Are the surest way
To meet the ludicrous
Future whose paths
Have been mislaid by
Psychopaths anyway,
So putting your best foot
Haywire and feeling
Hamstrung by knocking
Knees, go hoofing
Forward indefinitely
Before you break
Up at your own
Crossfooted horseplay
And resume your unofficial
Position: prone.

LAMENT FOR THE NON-SWIMMERS

They never feel they can be well in the water,
Can come to rest, that their bodies are light.
When they reach out, their cupped hands hesitate:
What they wanted runs between their fingers.
Their fluttering, scissoring legs sink under.

Their bones believe in heaviness, their ears
Shake out the cold invasion of privacy,
Their eyes squeeze shut. Each breath,
Only half air, is too breath-taking.
The dead-man's float seems strictly for dead men.

They stand in the shallows, their knees touching,
Their feet where they belong in the sand.
They wade as carefully as herons, but hope for nothing
Under the surface, that wilderness
Where eels and sharks slip out of their element.

Those who tread water and call see their blurred eyes
Turn distant, not away from a sky's reflection
As easy to cross as the dependable earth
But from a sight as blue as drowned men's faces.
They splash ashore, pretending to feel buoyant.

xxx

EPITAPHS

For a Math Student

His days were numbered. Here lies a digital tyro
Totalled, letting X be the unknown,
Cross-multiplying, equating himself with zero,
Learning at length the root of minus one.

For a Comedian

Here lies a stand-up comic, on his first
Unlimited engagement, playing it dead-pan,
Playing it low and blue, under-rehearsed,
With four chiselled one-liners, a straight man.

For a Dog Trainer

He strained at his leash and whined, but Death said, "Heel!"
And he heeled. "Sit!" and he sat. "Stay!" and he stayed.
When Death said, "Come!" he came, obedient, faithful,
Anxious to play. "Play dead!" Death said, and he played.

For a Midget

He knew his life would be short: that's how it began.
Others grew up, but he stayed undersize,
Freaked out in an outsize world, not called a man.
Look down on him now: he was used to downcast eyes.

For a Grammarian

Here, parsed forever in a complete sentence
With no independent clause, with no direct
Object among other neuter pronouns,
Without an active verb, without a subject . . .

For a Nudist

He shed his clothes, believing nothing should lie
Between his skin and the sun. Now nothing does
But grass and dirt and steel and mahogany
And satin and wool and polyester and moss.

TO THE FLY IN MY DRINK

You wouldn't listen to my wordless temperance lecture —
        The back of my hand — but hovered
Over my glass, tempted, already groggy, and finally
        Plunged when I wasn't looking,
Were soaked before I could swizzle you out of this low dive.
        Your feathery nose for news,
Your magnetic legs, your agile acrobat's wings, and all
        Your myriad eyes have had it.
Here's mud in those eyes. This drink is on you, a libation poured
        With genuine regret
In a garden where some cold-sober slug will celebrate
        Your wake through the night.

TO A PANHANDLER WHO, FOR A QUARTER, SAID "GOD BLESS YOU"

You held out your hand, expecting (on the average) nothing.
But when I crossed your palm with copper in an alloy sandwich
Newly minted by God's Country, you laid a misfortune
On me not even a prime-time gypsy would have thought of.

God bless *me? Me* be one for the cloud-capped, holy-
For-showbiz, smug, sharkskinny, hog-certain, flowery Chosen
Harping for glory? Thumbs-upping glissandos on pure-gold G-strings?
I couldn't stagger, let alone clodhop, to such music.

You could have said, *Heaven tempers the wind to the shorn lamb*
Or *Heaven will protect the working girl* or *Heaven*
Lies about us in our infancy. I half-swallowed those saws
Once. Their teeth stuck in my craw. Now I take wisdom sidewise.

Shorn lambs and working girls and infants over the years
Have taught me something else about Heaven: it exists
Maybe when the Corner-cutting Fleecer, the Punch
With the Time-clock, and the Unmilkable Mother aren't looking.

If God knows what's good for Him, He won't listen to you
About my anointment. He'll oil some squeakier sinner
And pour me an ordinary straight-up natural disaster.
Here's two-bits more, palmer, to hope I'll be worth a damn.

BEING HERDED PAST THE PRISON'S HONOR FARM

The closer I come to their huge black-and-white sides, the less
Room there is in the world for anything but Holsteins.
I thought I could squeeze past them, but I'm stuck now
Among them, dwarfed in my car, while they plod gigantically
To pasture ahead of me, beside me, behind me, cow eyes
As big as eightballs staring down at another prisoner.

They seem enormously pregnant, bulging with mash and alfalfa,
But their low-slung sacks and rawboned high-rise rumps look insur-
Mountable for any bull. One side-swipes my fender
And gives it a cud-slow look. What fingers would dare
Milk those veiny bags? Not mine. I'm cowed. My hands
On the steering wheel are squeezing much too tight to be trusted.

They all wear numbers clipped to their ears. They're going to feed
Behind barbed wire like a work-gang or, later, like solitaries
Stalled in concrete, for the milk of inhuman kindness.
They clomp muddily forward. Now splatting his boots down
Like cowflops, the tall black numbered trusty cowpoke tells me
Exactly where I can go, steering me, cutting me out of the herd.

SHADOW

Mine is falling beside me, a right-angle
Taking my measure by the slant of the sun.
He sifts through grass, encloses whole beds of flowers,
A masked marvel on the face of disaster:
Being run over or stomped, recklessly climbing
Up cliffs, over railings, floating unfathomably
On water, being flung head under heels
Down rocky slopes where he takes the rough with the smooth
Like the light denied him, his surrounding absence.

We meet underfoot at dawn and stretch
Together, but off he goes incredibly further,
A stilted balancing-act, who slowly shrinks,
Hardened by noon, to a circus dwarf,
A macrocephalic, blunt, prognathous partner
Clowning and cloggily nimble, squeezing to nothing
Under me, a hole in my ground, but tossing himself
Away toward distant matters again
In the nimbus of sunset, grimly bony.

By nightfall he's gone. The daytime prisoner
Escapes his keeper, completely unhinged
From his obligation to be all things to one man.
But sometimes suddenly leaping out of hiding
Behind my back by firelight, he flickers
With jagged, abrupt abandon
Through bushes and trees, an outsized marauder

Plunging through deeper shadows, threatening
At the edge of sleep to disappear forever.

Each morning he slips back with perfect timing
And waits for me to do anything — flop or flounder,
Even race. The end is always a dead heat.
I'll fall in that dead heat someday, no longer
Insanely predictable, to wait for *him*
To swivel upright, while a glare of darkness
Dawning beyond a vertical horizon
Casts my light substance — all my light bones
And lighter flesh — into his shadow play.

PILE-DRIVER

Listen, it says, I lunge
Downward one heavy head-fall
Deeper, making your shut windows
Rattle because this sludge is too
Muddled for your good, I butt
Downright with a huff of headlong
Battering like a ram and, hovering,
Drop as straight as I know how to
Thud on this sinking quivering
Pile-head because all earth must stay
Still in its place, in fixed
Order and not go lurching
Slantwise in wallows, sideslipping
Everything suddenly out from under
You who need so many more steady
Thumps on your stamping ground.

MEDITATION ON THE UNION BAY GARBAGE FILL

There would be classrooms here by now if the inspired garbage
(Fifty years of waste dumped by our City Fathers)
Hadn't stayed alive, sending its swamp gas
Through cracks and hummocks to flicker blue in the night, turning
Golf tees on the driving range into bunsen burners.

Already it's my classroom: I lunch here with marsh hawks
And chipping sparrows, quails and cinnamon teals, and listen
For something beyond the burr of traffic, having done my share
Of adding to this rubble over my years and years,
Of laying this foundation for wildlife.

The sign says it's a sanctuary. Dogs must be kept on leashes.
On mine, I stare at the tentative grass, a place for hard times
Where whatever wants to grow will have to make it
In the worst way, wrestling for root-room in gravel and broken glass
Or clawing and singing dead to rights for a nesting ground.

I wait my turn, a man grown desperate to be grown,
To be filled, to be fulfilled before it's too late
Even to hope for a sign from barn swallows, these masters
Of aimless, unpremeditated, single-minded grace, now flying
Carelessly through barbed wire, diving and doubling

Back at their own moment's notice over the yellow broom
And skimming across the crows' hodge-podgy gambits,
Their forked tails more delicate and precise than the glance of an eye

That can only follow the blue sheen of their curvetting
After the fact, hopelessly laggard but still dreaming

Here in the half-dead of summer
Of taking their ways above this flammable earth.

SEEDS

By night they climbed the dead sunflower stalks in my workroom
Like a circus act: the fieldmice, making their own percussion
Among dry leaves, spotlit by car-light and starlight,
Juggling the seeds still left in those corollas, balancing
High against books, nibbling and hoarding, spilling their shells
Over stained manuscripts, their perches bowing, wavering
Further, still further. But I was no claque for an encore.

So the sunflowers had to go. They suffered the last dust
To be knocked out of their roots, then trailed me to their birthplace,
A sundeck, where I shucked their seeds into a sack.
Their stalks and crook-necks had toughened through years of performi
As emblems of constant, hard-headed, sun-filled brooding
For this paper-scratcher who stared at them each morning, hoping
To learn their ways. I buried them over the side in a sea of ivy.

Now a pair of chickadees is at work on those same seeds.
They eat their fill and hide the rest in wild places
Where they'll sprout in the next rain: the cracks of furniture,
Under saucers, in bamboo blinds, behind peeling birchbark,
In the vacant eyes of a horse-skull, in a whale's backbone.
Black-and-white birds, the color of sunflower seeds and fieldmice,
Even ink and paper, are cramming darkness with light.

AFTER READING TOO MANY POEMS, I WATCH A ROBIN TAKING A BATH

For James Wright

She does it so devotedly
In the middle of her most ecstatic spasm
There seems to be no water
In the murky birdbath at all.

It's all in the air
At once, all showering above
Her paddling wings or running
Among her feathers spread like fingers.

She crouches, puffs the white down
Of her underbreast as if settling
On something pale blue, and the water gathers
Beneath her, against her.

Now she thinks a long moment
Without thinking, stares
North and south at the same time
At nothing.

And suddenly she's all done with it,
Up on the dripping edge, shaking
And sleek, alert, herself again,
Flying into hiding.

THAWING A BIRDBATH ON NEW YEAR'S DAY

At the crack of dawn my feet are crackling
Where the lawn in the night turned into broken glass
As the year turned over harder than ever.

While I pour it into the moss-lined, frozen birdbath,
The kettle is still whistling its only note
With breath, like mine, a momentary ghost.

The ice breaks into stars among dead leaves.
I shiver back to our house under cedar boughs
And watch them for an hour from a warm room:

The other whistlers who spent the night somewhere
Puffed out in thickets, in their brittle shelters,
Now starting late to drink the New Year in,

The finches and fox sparrows, the jays and towhees,
Some waiting for their share among stiff roses
Whose branches they learned by heart all through the summer.

If anything's worth remembering in that garden,
They know it, without petals, down to the thorns,
Down to both sides of leaf-like skeletons.

Slowly the ice comes back, feathery, thin.
They scatter out of sight through blackberries
And holly and bare lilac and morning glory.

It's the year's turn. Now we've drunk together,
Looking both ways from two-faced January —
From the cold to the cold — whistling to celebrate.

SITTING BY A SWAMP

Minutes ago, it was dead:
This swamp when I first came
Fell still as if poisoned,
The air expiring, cattails
Bent and brought to nothing
By the motionless water.

Now first the sunfish rising
To touch the underface
Of the pool, a muttered frog-call,
And out of the willow roots
From crushed stems and stubble
The chap of a marsh wren,

From a thicket a fox sparrow
Taking me in, one eye
At a wary time, where I wait
To be what they want me to be:
Less human. A dragonfly
Burns green at my elbow.

CUTTING DOWN A TREE

Having picked your tree and cleared its base of suckers,
You size it up roughly, looking as toplofty
As it, deciding now which way it should topple
By the lay of the land or its own inclination,
Even walking off the bed-ground, where you will put it
In its place for bucking and scaling, to make certain
No hidden stumps or cross-fallen logs
Will shatter it and cost you half your profit.

Now you must face it, taking your flat cut
And your steep undercut on the unsafe side,
Removing a wedge through one-third of its years.
For practical purposes, your tree is dead
At that moment, so making your back cut
(Level and higher) shouldn't weigh heavily
On what may be left of your uneasiness
At undertaking to saw through living heartwood.

It isn't your fault, is it? You walked on planks
All your half-life without thinking
Anything about it, nailed them, sat on them,
Pounded them with your fists or burned them
To soothe your aching forebrain with smoke and embers,
And you lay boxed by so many board feet
Each night, you could count your chips forever.
So call out *Timber* and forget all that.

Your tree will be starting to fall so slowly
You'll be tempted to think you have all the time

In the green world to get away, but now
You may have a problem: if your calculations
Haven't included an escape route
Which you've plotted carefully and trampled over —
Somewhere exempt from sitbacks and backfalls,
Skybinding, slabbing, and wild widowmakers —

Or if you've forgotten to clear all leaning snags,
The naturally dead with their punk knots and heart rot,
Which fall when the earth shakes (and you mean to shake it),
You could find yourself stuck in the undergrowth
With nothing to do but hope for the second best
And go (instead of forward) flat or backward
Into the sawdust of your expectations
With a mismanaged, butchered trunk or its dead brother

Dropping on you like a deadfall on a rabbit.

JUDGING LOGS

Among the horizontal trees (their branches
Gone, their roots and stumps
Gone to a slow end under blackberries)
The slow log-scaler
Strolls in the rain with his wand and his understanding
Pitiless eye,
Retracing the spiral scars of lightning, touching
Burl and ring shake,
Heart check and pitch spangle, deciding degrees
And shades of salvation:
What shall pass through circles of teeth to follow
The strait and narrow
Or what shall go up in smoke and down in ashes.
He is the resurrection
But lifeless, counting board feet, commanding
This flat last stand of cedars
Which once took crown-fire, windfall, and ice
As calmly as rain
But now, like the anonymous dead, take only
Numbers into the weather.

AN ADDRESS TO WEYERHAEUSER,
THE TREE-GROWING COMPANY

After miles of stumps and slash and the once-buried endeavors
Of roots, all dozer-bladed to their logical ends, the clear-cut
Ends finally at a stand of firs near a creek, and for an hour
I've listened to what's left of the winter wrens
Claiming the little they can for territory.

(Which isn't much. And I'm too mad to be lyrical about it,
Lacking their grace, their fearlessness, their ingenuity.
Let somebody else do it: one of the most beautiful songs
In North America, a long, wild, ringing melody,
Says *The Complete Fieldguide to American Wildlife*. It lasts
For seven seconds with sixteen distinct notes and sixteen stops
Per second, an amazing 112 notes, says *Life Histories*
Of North American Birds. Our machines can barely track them.)

One comes to scout me where I sit on the last stump
Before the forest holds out its dark-green light again.
He sings, watching me. There's no use trying to say
What the music is like, cascading out of this short-tailed genius
Smaller than a mouse. Another answers and another,
Distinct though distant. I catch a glimpse of one through glasses
Down by the creek. Being as scientific as the next-to-last man,
I mark the spot and measure it off on the deep soft forest floor
(No rhapsodic passages about licorice fern and running pine and moss)
As clumsily as a moon-walker. His voice was carrying
Clearly and easily five hundred feet and could have reached further,
But I'll stay reasonably sober: this tiny groundling,

This incredibly gifted ounce was moving and reclaiming
A hemisphere of June air weighing nine tons.

Mr. Weyerhaeuser, your fallers and heavy thinkers made this possible.
I realize June is a distracting month: you must trap and kill
All those ravenous black bears whose berries haven't ripened
And who maul and gnaw a few of your billions of saplings
And you're looking forward to spraying the already dying
Tussock moths again, regardless of our expense, regardless
Of what else may be trying to live under the branches,
But for a moment consider *troglodytes troglodytes*, this wren
Who has never forged a treaty or plotted a war
Or boasted of trying to serialize massacre after massacre
Or managed a forest or suffered the discomfort of an obituary
Listing credits in fraternal and charitable parlays
And other safe bets: he's moving a greater weight
Of living and dead matter daily than all your logging crews.
This creature smaller than your opposable thumb
And much more subtle is singing all day
In the woods you haven't clear-cut yet. Each song
Lasts seven seconds and forever. Think what you might manage
To move if you could sing or even listen.

AT THE EDGE OF A CLEAR-CUT FOREST

This rubble, pitched and jackstrawed to the horizon,
Was a forest deep enough to be lost in,
Taller than power-poles, where the only sounds
Were what it said to itself in the wind,
The rush of a stream, the cries of tree-frogs, birdsong,
The drummings of grouse, ground-squirrels' piercing warnings.

Four years ago, trucks hauled it away.
Now at the edge of this cemetery,
People have driven for miles in other trucks
To strew their junk among the stumps in the rain,
And here the men and boys with shotguns and rifles
Come day after day, loaded, primed to unload.

They shoot their starry holes in TV screens,
Slam-bang refrigerators, repuncture beercans,
Let stoves have it right in the oven doors,
Make sitting ducks out of bottles and plastic jugs,
Riddle the stuffing out of car-seats, plug away
And plug away at it till they're empty —

As empty as these miles where nothing is new,
Not the rain or the guns returning aimlessly
Or this stump speech. But there in a wheel-rut,
In a puddle beyond it through the spiralling
Remnants of box-springs among flooded roots,
The tadpoles swim, transforming themselves, persisting.

BUCK FEVER

When you see over your open sights the one sight
You've been aiming for
In the woods through your first hunting season,
You may find yourself
Unable to pull the trigger. You've dressed the part,
Cleaned and loaded
Your rifle, driven for miles and taken some good
Jolts to keep your wits
Alert (your lightest equipment), spent all the stealth
Your uninitiated craft
Could muster, even daydreamed of doing it:
The clean shot
Straight to the skull or the heart that could enlarge
You in your keen eyes
To a keen-eyed masterful self, and you're staring now
At the end of all that:
This deer, which is staring back to know you
And what you're standing for,
Slender and soundless, light-hoofed, wary, motionless —
That's beautiful.
Grimly, you brace the stock, your finger needing
Only to move
A shaky fraction to change you into a hunter.
If you hear an explosion
While sweating it out and see your trophy leaping
And slumping to its knees
And coughing blood and falling, then lying still,
You may learn to like it,

But if you choose (like it or not)
To remain silent
And your game escapes before your eyes, before
Your very eyes can believe
Your sure-fire methods have failed, your suffering
Will soon be over.
You must settle for second chances: laughing it off
Or swearing yourself sober,
You can stalk away for good, crackling and whistling,
Enjoying buck fever
And even thinking of coming back someday,
Disarmed, to recover.

DUCK-BLIND

Having prepared yourself
Seriously now for the serious
Business of hunting —
Your coat on crossed sticks
Set flapping at the flyway's
Crucial turn, your decoys
(The wooden coots and geese,
The dabblers and divers) spread
In the tried and tested
Worm-on-a-hook pattern
To cradle open water,
And yourself well hidden
Here in your duck-blind,
Your whole body
And what warms it blended
Naturally with the marsh,
With the drabness of dying
Reeds and widgeon grass,
Even the alien whiteness
Of your face net-masked or painted —
You are finally ready
To call those webfeet down
The echelon of the wind,
To lead your flock with foresight
And hindsight, breaking their wingbeats
Through a reddening hailstorm
With outburst after outburst
Against the light, marking their fall

Most watchfully with an eye
To harvesting the dead,
But recalling the wounded
Must never simply be wasted
Though they may dive and cling
To the roots of eelgrass, holding
Their breath for a last time
Far longer than you think
You can possibly wait. Waiting
And growing cold, you aim
Down through the quivering water.
You wait for them to rise.

SETTING A SNARE

Your problem is getting a small game animal
To trust your world
(Which he thinks is his) just long enough to be
Yanked away from it.
Like you, he's fond of walking old paths and playing
Safe under cover,
So framing his trail with wire and a bent sapling
Hair-triggered by sticks,
You can offer a passage under a fallen log
And into a gallows
More natural-seeming than any common hangman's:
He knows all trees
Have a way of falling, that saplings may look crippled,
And he's slipped through
Strand after strand elsewhere without a slipknot.
If you're sure the setting
Seems innocent enough to pass his furtive senses,
Then make this noose
Be you in your absence, performing without flinching
The act of strangling.
Ideally, when you come back, you will have missed
The unpleasant details,
Which needn't bother us now, and will find harmless
What hangs there and hangs there.
Out of reach of the other animals, it waits
For you and you alone.

TRAPLINE

Running your trapline through the woods — the miles of sets
By burrows and den-logs, at the lips of streams —
You turn bone-tired,
Sleeping a little better now than when you kept dreaming
Wolves, bears, and all that restless nonsense
You can't help
Troubling yourself about till you're cured of being alone
Like a prime skin. It was hard learning to think
At all like an animal,
To outsmart even the most careless marten or gray fox,
Ermine or otter, but harder now to quit,
To act without feeling
Sorry for what you have to go through to deserve their hides:
They won't give in when they're caught, won't make it easy.
They'd rather cripple themselves
By biting away the last shreds of a paw while waiting
For you. But now you're getting used to it,
Approaching the sprung traps
Without exactly shrinking, facing those teeth and those eyes
That almost stop you cold.
Now you know
What you have to do: the handgun-shot, the knife-slash or garrotte
As businesslike as possible, then skinning
(All ways are hard
So never mind), fleshing, and salting, the quick throwaway
Of what was inside the fur, which should look ravishing
Over some lady's shoulder

As she shows all her teeth to the one who catches her.
You wash your red hands then in freezing water,
Watching it run away
Into the clear, as free and pure as it ever was
Before you touched it, while you're rebaiting
(With a ripe offering)
Your steel-spring swivel-chained offset leg-hold moneymaker
For the next go-round. This is a good life,
Isn't it? — all this
Fresh air and breathing easy, breathing over and over
As much as you like, catching your breath
As many times as you want to.

POSING WITH A TROPHY

Lying on the ground, your bear
Or cougar will look small, no matter
Where you stand in the picture,
Even putting your foot
In a time-honored position
On its carcass. Your trophy
Will loom much larger
If hoisted into the air
By its hind legs (never
The front legs or the neck: it will loll
Backwards or seem to strangle).

What your future admirers
(Hopefully) will wish to see
Is what you had to do
With a dangerous predator.
Your place is the background
Where, by comparison, you'll appear
Smaller and more suitable
For framing, holding your rifle
At a casual angle, perhaps kneeling
To suggest reverent fatigue,
But above all never trying
To look more masterful
Than you are, simply aiming

A smile into the distance
Where good things come to an end.

A shot in living color
Under glass on the wall
Will share, like taxidermy,
Whatever shows on your face
(The teeth of the evidence)
As clearly, as speechlessly
As the snarl beside you.

✖✖✖

THE ORCHARD OF THE DREAMING PIGS

As rosy as sunsets over their cloudy hocks, the pigs come flying
Evening by evening to light in the fruit trees,
Their trotters firm on the bent boughs, their wings
All folding down for the dark as they eat and drowse,
Their snouts snuffling a comfortable music.

At dawn, as easily as the light, they lift
Their still blessed souse and chitlings through the warming air,
Not wedging their way like geese, but straggling
And curling in the sunrise, rising, then soaring downward
To the bloody sties, their breath turned sweet as apples.

XXX

WATERFALL

It plunges into itself, stone-white, mottled with emerald,
And finished falling forever, it goes on
Falling, half rain, to a pool
In bedrock and turns, extravagantly fallen, to recover
Its broken channel through maple and maidenhair
But always falling
Again, again, the same water, having been meanwhile
Everywhere under the moon, salted and frozen,
Thawed and upraised
Into its cloudy mother-of-pearl feathers to gather
Against the mountains, foregathering its own
And streaming once more
To fall as it must fall at the verge of understanding
In a roaring downpour as strange as this very moment
Swept over and over.

MAKING A FIRE IN THE RAIN

Rain has filled all these branches, living or broken,
And filled the river. I gather driftwood
And heap it on the stone-covered, shelving point
Where a man-sized backlog has beached itself,
And now the problem is obvious: nothing will burn
Willingly. Nothing wants to make fire but me.

Out of my half-remembered merit-badging,
I stack a pyramid of twigs and tinder,
Use myself as a lean-to, cheat with torn paper
And kitchen matches, and manage to start a flicker
That shifts, dodges, dies out, hisses, turns yellow,
Spits rain, reddens, then finally catches on.

I build it slowly toward branches thick as my arms
And cross them, smoking and steaming, over the heart.
I feed it and take Creator-Destroyer's pride
In this burning place, this point of consuming interest
Where my eyes follow each change of shape or color,
Direction or size, like an omen of pyromancy.

The backlog darkens: one hollow gives up the ghost
And shrinks to blackening cells, to cloistered charcoal.
It could have led dozens of other lives,
Been sawed or carved or pulped, stayed lost in the woods

To nurse new saplings and ferns, a bed for moss.
Instead, it starts a second death by fire.

Its leaves once hoarded the sun. That heat breaks out,
The river escapes it, sizzling, a stone explodes,
Rain slants, wind blusters among it, the flame huddles:
I share all these exchanges of elements,
Being pummelled by one and breathing still another
And sitting on the uncompromising third

And staring at the burnt crux of the fourth:
Fire and water and wind on this bare earth —
They know each other of old, even outside in,
But newcomers like me fumble among them
To search for Aqua Vitae, Philosopher's Stones,
The Inspiring Breath, the Refining Fire, Fool's Gold.

The rain is too much, suddenly, the wind deadly,
The stones too blunt, and the fire too close for comfort.
I get up no wiser, though now cured like a salmon,
And climb to the road, turning for one more look
At that obstinate tongue of light dwindling to nothing.
The smoke sweeps off downstream in a toppling column.

RETURN TO THE RIVER

Through streaming sunlight and rain, surging, the humpback salmon
Climb home again, fins cutting the swift water
From shallows to pools
And up long drifts to rapids, their beaklike jaws once more
Tasting the truth of their first and final spawning —
Among them, these three holding
Where a female on her side is flailing her body ragged
On the nesting stones, her sleek jade tail gone white
As the foam around her,
And the four all suddenly yielding, surrendering to the current,
Swerving and yawing faster than it downstream,
Rehearsing their deaths,
But as suddenly turning, returning, hovering (like gulls
Playing the wind's hard game), one scarred near the eye,
The round clear staring eye,
By a fisherman's gaff or a seal or the teeth of a killer whale
In the moons of his salt life, the female thrashing
Again and again at the nest,
And the falling alder leaves skimming among them, the sky
Falling in gray-blue pieces fluttering shoreward
Like a hatch of mayflies,
And the males all holding, swaying above and behind her, waiting
For days for their instant, while the sun sinks deep and rises,
Scattering salmon-light.

NIGHT SONG

Chiljilt, sichizi, gunjule, inzayu, ijanale.
— Apache prayer

At dawn, I found Dragonfly dying
Beside my path, far from water,
His blue needle stitching breath
To breath, catching at air
With the dry nets of his wings.
Now I lie by the same path, my fear
Beside me in darkness, breathing.
Night, be good, do not let me die.

At noon, in a circle of stones, I found
The breath-feather of Hawk.
He has fallen somewhere
To the mouths of his smallest brothers
Who will crawl out of the cracked earth
To steal his eyes, to take him
Where he has never flown before.
Night, be good, do not let me die.

At evening, West Wind fell.
Sun fell. Sky closed again.
The sharp small spilled water-filled song
Of Wren went dry as my mouth.
The open yellow-and-white hands
Of Cactus Woman gathered to fists.
Now the fire's heart shrinks like my heart.
Night, be good, do not let me die.

Three

FINDING THE RIGHT DIRECTION

Those times when too much stands between you and the sky —
Tree crowns and clouds or mist — when the hidden sun
Makes nothing of your shadow
To guide you south, you turn to stones, to slopes and trees,
To flowers, even to birds for your directions:
Cutting across bedrock,
The scars of glacial drift all point the same hard way
To mark the graveyard of ice which trundled boulders
Grindingly up hills
And, gouging abrupt drop-offs, tumbled them over and over
And left them strewn like markers, blunt in smooth fields,
While it melted south
On one straight, glittering journey which you may follow now
Rejoicing toward the end of your own ice age,
Sunbound and shrinking,
Or if the brush grows dense and your unmindful eyes
Can't choose between the dextrous and sinister,
See, the lightest branches,
The thickest, hardest bark most deeply grooved, the heaviest
Roots of old trees will stand to the bitter north,
Braced against winter,
And even the newly dead will show where not to go:
The center of decay lies out of sunlight.
Young trees lean *with* you
Like the new grass in this clearing where you've stumbled, seeing
Wildflowers sharing your clouds, but staring southward
For the certain return
Of what once brought them to light and, look, this empty cabin

At the edge of it, unhinged by years of weather,
Has under the southern eaves
Your surest compass, expecting a break in the gray of morning:
A swallow's nest clinging to next to nothing
Like you, beginning now.

WALKING IN BROKEN COUNTRY

Long after the blossoming of mile-wide, fire-breathing roses
In this garden of dead gods when Apache tears
Burst out of lava
And after the crosshatched lightning and streambeds cracking
Their sideslips through mid-rock, after burnishing wind,
Your feet are small surprises:
Lurching down clumps of cinders, unpredictably slipshod,
And gaining your footholds by the sheerest guesswork,
You make yourself at home
By crouching, by holding still and squinting to puzzle out
How to weave through all this rubble to where you're going
Without a disaster:
One dislocation, one green-stick fracture, and all your bones
May fall apart out of sympathy forever.
In this broken country
The shortest distance between two points doesn't exist.
Here, straight lines are an abstraction, an ideal
Not even to be hoped for
(As a crow flies, sometimes) except on the briefest of terms:
Half a step on legs, after which you slump,
Swivel, or stagger.
You cling to surfaces feebly in a maze without a ceiling,
A whole clutch of directions to choose among
From giddy to earthbound,
Where backtracking from dead-ends is an end in itself.
Through this clear air, your eyes put two and two
Together, take them apart,

And put them together again and again in baffling pieces,
Seeing the matter of all your sensible facts
Jumbled to the horizon.

CLIMBING ALONE

Against your own judgment, you begin climbing these rocks,
Using your grudging, shaky extremities
For footholds and handholds
In a school of hard knocks where kneecaps, crazybones, skull,
Even coccyx, demand your strictest attention:
They must take new postures
Slowly and surely enough to keep your center of gravity
From getting above itself and joining rock slides.
The joys of mass wasting
In the wrong direction are better left to minerals
At which you stare up close, highly concerned
With their good health,
Their age and strength, their disposition, their failures,
And the likelihood of their remaining with you
When you cling to them.
You don't look down or back: for the purposes of falling,
A little distance is as good as a mile.
It goes a long, long way
To nowhere, putting your body permanently out of condition.
You brace up a chimney, right-angled, steeping yourself
In the history of stress,
But when you stop to think or breathe, as you must, to perform
The necessary functions of not fainting
And not losing your mind,
Your best intentions seem more ludicrous than usual.
At the height of your foolishness you remember why
On earth you wanted to do this

And find it unfathomably strange, seeing coiled beside you
Your rope with nothing at the end of it
But the end of it.

CROSSING A RIVER

You kneel on the verge of this impassable arroyo,
Filled now with a river instead of easy dust,
And drink it in
Literally, pumice and all, not from the sealed lips
Of your canteen but, to celebrate, from your hands,
And watch it surging
Between you and the impossible place you had meant to go,
Past a stream like a stairway, flooded and broken
At the foot of a monument
To the greater glory of stones, all cutbanks and no point bars,
A torrent not to be forded if you can't stand
The equal partnership
Of branches, rocks, and whole bushes, its leapfrogging bedload,
Which would carry you off and lose you without a murmur.
You could sit down
And eventually it would dwindle, falter, and go away
Like a second thought failing before your eyes,
Or you could climb,
Maybe, scraping your way up cliffs to its source, finding nothing,
No fountainhead to circle and mull around
Or to turn young by,
Just seasonally bad weather running off cloudy spillways.
So you head downstream on the good side of it,
Trying to get somewhere
The way *it* does: temporarily. This scarred, unearthly ravine
May be someone's, and the fullness thereof, but not yours,
Not even this river's
For long, as it makes up its mind about the weakness

Of what lies under it, what to carry away,
What course to choose
While glancing toward gravity, making no grand progress
And not resounding through multi-colored canyons
But disappearing
Abruptly with all its rainwash in a flattening fan
In the dry silt of the playa beside you
Where, if you've played along,
You'll find your eyes intent on a different level, not broken
Yet, where water goes underground without you.
Here you are free to cross.

STANDING IN THE MIDDLE OF A DESERT

You stop halfway in this bleakness to reconsider
Everything underfoot,
Which, like white sunlight and the punishing air,
Seems in favor of dying.
You don't have enough essential qualities
To vegetate here:
You may be distorted, bitter, fleshy, and smooth,
But not well armored,
Not deeply or widely rooted, gray-green, or dwarfish.
An executioner
Like that crook-backed creosote whose poisonous roots
Kill its own seedlings
(Unless some unlikely rain leaches the earth)
Has one idea: its life.
But if you stayed still and tried to be self-effacing,
You'd bear numberless offspring
Whose sincerest flattery wouldn't be imitation
But helping themselves to you:
They'd be overjoyed to live on your behalf,
Leave nothing to waste,
Leave nothing at all to your imagination,
So you have to move,
Marking your time in this intractable sand,
More footloose than ever.

XXX

AT THE POINT OF NO RETURN

Till now, you could have taken back your steps
Like slips of the foot:
They were turning points where, more easily than not,
You could have given up,
Gone back to the start, forgotten, tried something different.
But from here on
It will take more courage to turn than to keep going.
You take two strides,
Each boot on its own, and you're headed one way only,
Irresponsibly committed,
Refreshed by the absence of the power to choose.
You enjoy believing
Your tracks in the blowing sand (that dusty mulch
Protecting deeper water)
May offer for an hour thousands of shelters,
Small rooting places
For seeds that, without you, would have kept on tumbling
Unfulfilled downwind,
So your line of march, no matter how misdirected
By your fixed or wandering
Star-sighted, red-rimmed eyes, may be remembered
By an equally erratic,
Interrupted, and inexplicable line of survivors,
Which till their last season
Will be straining root and branch taller than dunes
To postpone their burial.

LIVING OFF THE LAND

Your eyes gnaw at the land ahead for food. You travel
Light-headed, ravenous, your jaws rehearsing
Zigzagging ruminations,
Grindings, incisive choppings, those broad-minded habits
That make you omnivorous by reputation
But in name only:
Here, in the desert, your natural disadvantages
Come into focus better than your eyes —
A rank amateur's nose,
A lack of teeth ridged well enough for the mangling of thorns,
Shortness of daily range, shortness of breath,
The griping of your guts
At the half-thought of settling for carrion like the vultures
Now effortlessly hanging-fire around you,
Concerned for your welfare.
You know what coyotes know: sheep may not safely graze
With or without a shepherd near your hunger.
But being a scavenger
Means learning to skulk till carcasses and the time seem ripe.
The relative deadness of flesh depends on timing
As much as taste
Unfortunately for you, whose hungry, impatient ancestors
Survived (in a world where bones grew popular)
By being and tasting terrible:
At best, you would be last in line at communal dinners
Under this meat-loving sun, or the last of your line
At the dead head of it.
If you look under your feet, whose shrinking, hardening shadows

Match every step you take, burnt black by sunlight,
You see you could grub there
Or grovel for one more grubstake, kneeling, praying for seeds
(If any nearby have had decent burial)
To sprout and bear fruit,
But for you it's a waiting game that might take generations
To master: all the lost seasons, all the clouds
That never arrive
Except in their own good time, when you, having drifted off,
Might not remember what every seed remembers:
What it is.
You'd have turned into all you can eat, this air and this sand,
Faltering, flowing even without water
Uneventfully downwind.

READING THE LANDSCAPE

You sit and breathe, scanning the raw illusions of distance
And nearness for the lay of this land, depending
On what you are,
A pivot casting the only restless shadow for miles.
Far off, the horizon traces its own downfall —
Mountainous once,
The wrack of living seas, steep fire, a storming of stones,
Now slowly settling for less under the weather,
That fearless explorer
Of weakness in the bindings of mind and matter. Nearby, lost ice
Through freeze and thaw has cracked a granite causeway
Where gnarled manzanita
Has made one fault its own, has wrestled for root-room,
And now bears fruit you share with unknown neighbors.
You feel strangely at home
In the visible world, a place called Here and There, on the seat
Of kings, the gluteus maximus, deluded
Into thinking you're not lost
At the heart of this bewilderment. Your only shelters
Are half-shut eyes and a shut mouth, but sandgrains
(Once firm rock, now shattered)
Have entered those three rooms, sharing your misunderstandings
Of what you say and see, reminding you
Your mind's voice and mind's eye
Are equally vulnerable in their pastimes and desolations,
Their taste for all the flavors of light and shade
And the sweet nothings
Of casual, elaborate, or desperate speech. Your duties

Are to rest and be recreated, then to stand,
Ignoring all directions
But your own, and to exercise your freedom of chance by aiming
Somewhere, keeping a constant Here beside you
As faithfully as your death.

SEEING THINGS

Browbeaten by the sun,
Squinting, and long since out of focus yourself
In a sharp-edged, keen-eyed world, you take whatever looms
Or lords it over you
Or spills its rippling lakes across this desert
More placidly than those expecting to feel cold sober.
You know that shimmer of water
Isn't for you, will keep a critical distance
Like grazing antelope sidling from your approaches.
You know that heavenly mansion
Hanging upside down or having it both ways
To a pinnacle is a shack or boulder beyond the horizon
Where you would spend hard times.
You know the delectable mountains like layer cakes
Are twice as far away as they seem and completely inedible.
But your fondness for light,
For the earth's unlimited metamorphoses,
Should help you go along with its disguises, shifting
(But not uneasily)
The burden of proof to the eyes of other beholders
Who don't know what you are, who may be seeing you now
As a menacing, blurred afrit,
A towering apparition wobbling toward them
Helplessly, their last hope, their disillusionment.

LYING AWAKE IN A DESERT

Displaced by darkness, you lie flat on your back,
Putting the world behind you, and stare at the moon,
The embarrassing moon, with nothing to offer it,
No ebb or flow, no wolfish transformations
Except this lunacy you keep to yourself.

You feel defenseless at last — no choice of weapons
And no opponent, only a field of honor,
This sand where you make little or no impression,
Though it takes you as you are, dead or alive,
As a kind of minor natural disaster.

If a sound should startle you out of your unsound sleep,
Whistling, buzzing, or droning, wingbeats, scuttling
Of small dry claws, lie still. Nothing at night
Makes noise by accident. If you hear, you were meant to
Or the indifferent source has found you harmless.

No matter how cold you feel to yourself, your colleagues —
The scorpions, sidewinders, and spiny swifts —
Will come to share the benefit of your body
And its residual heat. They'll lie beside you
More trustingly than you could with a stranger.

So if you wake in the morning, do it gently,
One eye, one branch, one thought, one stretch at a time,
Being a homing place and point of departure.
Meanwhile, get through this night of reckoning
By the irrational riches of starlight.

LOOKING FOR WATER

At the lip of your canteen, kissing that last sure drop
Goodbye, you choose the least unlikely direction —
Hills (if there are any)
Or greenness (if there is such a shade) or somewhere familiar
(If you can remember how some map unfolded
For your civilized fingers
By artificial light) — or barring those choices, anywhere.
You're keeping cool in spite of the persuasions
Of the surrounding air,
The parched ground burning underfoot, the sun too thirsty
Now that you're living by the sweat of your brow.
You watch for clouds
Like a furrow-faced, drought-plagued farmer ready to hire
The dry wits of witches, cannons of rainmakers,
Or prayers made of sand.
Though they make no streambed for that smallest of tributaries
Under your tongue, you put small stones in your mouth
For their durable comfort
But, with what remains of your breath, practice no oratory
Here in this speechless country, wasting no words
On self-absorbed cacti:
Though you behead one, crush its pale pulpy heart, squeeze out
Briefly what it had saved through fifty summers,
And leave it dying,
Your graying stubble drains off no excess heat like its needles,
And your blundering, rootless sense of territory
Can't match its self-possession.
You may find, by growing or fading light, a waterhole

With genuine liquid filling a charmed circle
Before your very knees,
But if nothing green surrounds it, one slip of the tongue,
One head-first impulse, and you may leave yourself
In a roofless mortuary,
Yet if suddenly real bushes are offering real leaves
Or if at the foot of a hill you find seep willows
Or anything blooming
In a dry creekbed or lakebed, or if you can listen hard,
Not to the ragged pulse in your mind's ear
(That deserted music)
For the actual droning of bees, for actual birdsong, and can follow
To the place where they've made their lives over and over,
Where deer-flies hover
Green and gold above damp sand or clay, start digging.
Wait by that emptiness. If it trickles and fills,
Your luck is only beginning.
The flies and bees will join you in that bitter communion,
Will take it with you, as drunk as true believers
Sharing another kingdom.

GETTING THERE

You take a final step and, look, suddenly
You're there. You've arrived
At the one place all your drudgery was aimed for:
This common ground
Where you stretch out, pressing your cheek to sandstone.
What did you want
To be? You'll remember soon. You feel like tinder
Under a burning glass,
A luminous point of change. The sky is pulsing
Against the cracked horizon,
Holding it firm till the arrival of stars
In time with your heartbeats.
Like wind etching rock, you've made a lasting impression
On the self you were
By having come all this way through all this welter
Under your own power,
Though your traces on a map would make an unpromising
Meandering lifeline.
What have you learned so far? You'll find out later,
Telling it haltingly
Like a dream, that lost traveller's dream
Under the last hill
Where through the night you'll take your time out of mind
To unburden yourself
Of elements along elementary paths
By the break of morning.
You've earned this worn-down, hard, incredible sight

Called Here and Now.
Now, what you make of it means everything,
Means starting over:
The life in your hands is neither here nor there
But getting there,
So you're standing again and breathing, beginning another
Journey without regret
Forever, being your own unpeaceable kingdom,
The end of endings.

✸✸✸

ACKNOWLEDGMENTS

Some of the poems in this volume have been previously published in the following: American Poetry Review ("Finding the Right Direction"), Antaeus ("Thawing a Birdbath on New Year's Day"), The Atlantic ("Part Song," "Ode to the Muse on Behalf of a Young Poet," "Lament for the Non-swimmers," "Pile-driver," "Return to the River"), Blue Buildings ("At the Edge of a Clear-cut Forest," "Getting There"), Carolina Quarterly ("To the Fly in My Drink"), Chicago Review ("Cloudburst," "Meditation on the Union Bay Garbage Fill"), Field ("Into the Nameless Places"), The Georgia Review ("Climbing Alone"), Graham House Review ("For a Woman Who Said Her Soul Was Lost"), Hampden-Sydney Poetry Review ("Standing in the Middle of a Desert," "At the Point of No Return"), Hudson Review ("Love Song After a Nightmare," "Book Sale — Five Cents Each!"), Kayak ("Stunts"), Massachusetts Review ("Making a Fire in the Rain," "Living Off the Land"), The New Yorker ("My Father's Wall," "Seeds," "Sitting by a Swamp"), Ohio Review ("Walking in Broken Country"), Oregon East ("Looking Up"), Paris Review ("The Junior Highschool Band Concert"), Poetry ("Thistledown," "Elegy While Pruning Roses," "The Death of the Moon," "The Gift," "Elegy for a Minor Romantic Poet," "Being Herded Past the Prison's Honor Farm," "To a Panhandler Who, for a Quarter, Said 'God Bless You'," "After Reading Too Many Poems, I Watch a Robin Taking a Bath," "Cutting Down a Tree," "Crossing a River," "Seeing Things"), Poetry in the Cities: Snohomish County Arts Council ("Night Song"), Poetry Miscellany ("An Address to Weyerhaeuser, the Tree-growing Company," "Buck Fever," "Duck-blind"), Portland Review ("The Singers"), Prairie Schooner ("Songs My Mother Taught Me," "Watching the Harbor Seals," "For a Woman Who Dreamed All the Horses Were Dying"), Raccoon ("Epitaphs"), Salmagundi ("Reading the Landscape," "Lying Awake in a Desert"), Shenandoah ("Judging Logs"), Southern Review ("Trapline"), Times Literary Supplement ("Boy Jesus," "Setting a Snare," "Posing with a Trophy," "The Orchard of the Dreaming Pigs," "Looking for Water"), Western Humanities Review ("After the Speech to the Librarians," "Jeremiad," "Dirge for a Player-piano," "My Flying Circus," "Waterfall," "Shadow").